JESUS, OUR ANCHOR

#2 in the *Live Anchored* Bible Study Series

Katie Robertson

"We have this hope [Jesus] as an anchor for the soul, firm and secure."

Hebrews 6:19

Jesus, Our Anchor
First Edition Trade Book
Copyright © 2019 by Katie Robertson

All rights reserved. No part of this publication may be reproduced, stored in a system, or transmitted in any form by any means—electronic, mechanical, photocopy, recording, or otherwise—except for brief quotations in critical or articles, without the prior permission of the publisher, except as provided copyright law.

Unless otherwise marked, Scriptures are taken from the Holy Bible, New International Version®, NIV®. Copyright © 1973, 1978, 1984, 2011 by Biblica, Inc.™ Used by permission of Zondervan. All rights reserved worldwide. www.zondervan.com. The "NIV" and "New International Version" are trademarks registered in the United States Patent and Trademark Office by Biblica, Inc.™

Scripture quotations marked NLT are from the New Living Translation, copyright ©1996, 2004, 2007, 2013, 2015 by Tyndale House Foundation. Used by permission of Tyndale House Publishers, Inc., Carol Stream, Illinois 60188. All rights reserved.

To order additional books, contact: katiejr@comcast.net
Or visit www.amazon.com

Or, visit Katie's website at www.liveanchored.com

ISBN: 978-1-7329092-3-6

Book development and production: Inspira Literary Solutions, Gig Harbor, WA
Book design: Brianna Showalter, Ruston, WA
Printed in the USA by IngramSpark, Nashville, TN

*Dedicated to Annika Joy, my extra special treasure.
Her kindred spirit and walk in faith continue to encourage me.*

We must anchor ourselves to the steadfast characteristics of God.
-Max Lucado

*The ultimate protection against sinking during life's storms
is devoting time to develop your friendship with Jesus.*
-Sarah Young

*Yet this I call to mind and therefore I have hope:
Because of the Lord's great love we are not consumed, for His compassions
never fail. They are new every morning; great is your faithfulness.
I say to myself, "The Lord is my portion; therefore I will wait for him."
The Lord is good to those whose hope is in him, to the one who seeks him;
it is good to wait quietly for the salvation of the Lord.*
Lamentations 3:21-25

TABLE OF CONTENTS

Introduction	9
How to Use This Study	13
Week One: **JESUS IS OUR FRIEND**	17
Week Two: **JESUS SHOWS US THE FATHER**	23
Week Three: **JESUS IS OUR LORD AND CAPTAIN**	31
Week Four: **JESUS IS OUR SHEPHERD**	39
Week Five: **JESUS IS OUR KING**	45
End of Study Wrap-Up	51
About the Author	55

Introduction

When I wrote my first book, *Anchored*, several years ago, I had no idea that it would signal the beginning of a series of Bible study books and a network of women's ministry gatherings by the same name. As it turns out, the desire to "live anchored" is a longing in the hearts of more people than I ever imagined.

These days, I am out frequently in various communities, speaking and interacting with women (and men and children too), sharing the story of how God has kept our own family anchored through times of grief and loss and tumult. As I share my own experiences, I hear dozens and dozens of similar stories. Different, but yet the same in many ways.

After all, life—for any of us—is full of stormy weather of varying degrees, from squalls to tsunamis. That's not just true of the weather; it's also true of life circumstances, and I have experienced my fair share of both. I am more convinced than ever that to navigate this life, we all need a Strong Anchor.

In our family's life, losing our 19-year old daughter, Karina Jean, to cancer in 2010 was the most devastating loss I'd ever experienced—and one I thought I could never bear. But with God's strength, we stood strong, and God is more real to us all than ever. Recently, we welcomed our first grandchild into our family, Isla Karina, born to Annika and Gray. She is truly a gift and amazing blessing to us all! What joy she has brought our whole family in the midst of our grief.

Because we are a boating family, I find imagery of the sea—and nautical style—rich and insightful, and very often metaphorical of many aspects of the Christian life. In particular, the metaphor of an anchor has become incredibly meaningful to me—and so very, very real.

Hebrews 6:19, which describes hope as an anchor for our soul, especially speaks to me. I know from owning a boat for many years how important the anchor is. A boat's anchor, though small in size compared to that of the vessel, is heavy enough to hold firm in the midst of a strong squall or storm. It is designed to grip into the bottom of the seabed so that even the strongest wind or current will not displace the boat or drive it onto the rocks.

I find this comparison—an anchor to hope in Jesus—vivid and profound. Following are four things that are true of an anchor in the world of boating, and that are equally true in our everyday lives. Along with these truths, I've included some questions for you to reflect on as we get started in this study, and as you consider how to anchor your life to the ultimate Anchor, Jesus Christ.

1. **You *must* have an anchor.** It is required by law that every boat have one.

   Using boating as an analogy for life, what is your anchor? What do you tend to place your hope, confidence, and security on?

2. **The anchor must be properly set.** It is very important to think about where to set the anchor. Set the anchor of Jesus and His truths in your heart. The Bible tells us, "Above all else guard your heart for out of it

is the wellspring of life" (Proverbs 4:23). The heart is where life starts, so anchoring your life on God's truths will bring you life.

Have you taken these truths from head knowledge to your heart? On a scale of 1 to 10, to what extent do you feel God's truths are set in your heart?

3. **Anchor in the calm before the storms hit.**

Are you currently experiencing a time of calm right now, or a time of storm? In what ways are you experiencing this? (Note: It's best to anchor in the calm but never too late to anchor in the storm!)

4. **Check the anchor.** We call this "Anchor Watch." This is a term that boaters use, and it is extremely critical in bad weather. It is extremely important that you make sure your boat doesn't move. And it is equally important to check for drifting once you are anchored.

What or whom do you have that encourages you in your faith journey, especially during the storms of life? Do you have someone who holds you accountable, or with whom you can check in? Do you have a community around you (family, friends, church, Bible study, etc.) that can help keep you encouraged and anchored in your life?

It is when we are securely anchored that we can begin to live life to the full—REAL life. This is what Jesus promised when He said, "The thief comes only to steal and kill and destroy; I have come that they may have life, and have it *to the full*" (John 10:10). Living life on God's promises will keep us strong and keep us from drifting. We can stand firm and live life to the full now and for eternity!

> *"We have this HOPE [Jesus] as an ANCHOR for the soul,*
> *firm and secure."* Hebrews 6:19

How to Use this Study

I've identified five truths about the strong characteristics of Jesus, and over the next five weeks, we're going to explore together how Jesus is the ultimate anchor for our life. These are amazing truths that, once set in our hearts in belief, will help us begin to live life to the full and be encouraged to live strong in this world!

Each week in your *Jesus, Our Anchor* lesson, you'll have the opportunity to:

1. Drop Anchor – hear a story of one of the five "anchor truths" about Jesus, and what it can mean to you
2. Get Your Bearings – explore what God's Word, the Bible, says about that anchor truth and start to fill yourself up with truth
3. Set the Anchor Truth in Your Heart – apply the truths you are learning from God's Word to your own life so you can start to live in the abundant life Jesus promised

When we are anchored to Jesus, we can endure; we can hold on to hope. And, we can experience God's peace, no matter what the circumstances. I know. I have experienced it. As of this writing, I have walked with Jesus for more than 40 years. In those years, I've experienced the exhilaration of clear skies and smooth sailing, and the anxiety and terror of high winds and stormy seas. Through it all, I've learned we need to have an anchor for our lives to keep us from being swept away, emotionally and/or spiritually, in any of the seasons of our lives. We have to set that anchor firmly in our hearts and begin to live and believe on the truths of God's word.

Here are the five anchor truths about Jesus that I want to impress on you through this study:

1. JESUS IS OUR FRIEND. "Greater love has no one than this, that he lay down his life for his FRIENDS. You are my FRIENDS if you do what I command. I no longer call you servants . . . Instead, I have called you FRIENDS, for everything that I learned from my Father I have made known to you." (John 15:13-15)

2. HE SHOWS US OUR FATHER. "See what great love the FATHER has lavished on us, that we should be called children of God! And that is what we are!" (1 John 3:1)

3. HE IS OUR LORD AND CAPTAIN. "Trust in the LORD with all your heart, and do not lean on your own understanding. In all your ways acknowledge Him, and He will make your path straight." (Proverbs 3:5-6)

4. HE IS OUR SHEPHERD. "The Lord is my SHEPHERD; I shall not want. He makes me lie down in green pastures. He leads me beside still waters. He restores my soul. He leads me in paths of righteousness for His name's sake. Even though I walk through the valley of the shadow of death, I will fear no evil for you are with me; your rod and your staff, they comfort me." (Psalm 23:1-4)

5. HE IS OUR KING. "You are a chosen people, a royal priesthood, a holy nation, a people belonging to God, that you may declare the praises of Him who called you out of darkness into His wonderful light." (1 Peter 2:9)

I hope you'll take time to ponder what it really means to have Jesus as an anchor. Before we begin, take a few minutes to answer these few self-reflection questions:

What does it mean to you personally to have Jesus as your ANCHOR?

_____
_____
_____
_____
_____

When did you first hear about how Jesus can be your ANCHOR? (Or have you never heard?) Can you remember when you decided to make Him the ANCHOR of your life? What do you remember about that time in your life and what it meant to you?

_____
_____
_____
_____
_____

If this is a new idea for you, and you have not yet decided to make Jesus your ANCHOR, what *does* anchor you in this life? (Think about both the storms and the calm times of life.)

If anything, what *prevents* you from trusting Jesus as your ANCHOR?

WEEK ONE

Jesus Is Our Friend

"Greater love has no one than this, that he lay down his life for his friends.
You are my friends if you do what I command.
I no longer all you servants…Instead, I have called you friends,
for everything I learned from my Father I have made known to you."
John 15:13-15

Drop Anchor

I came to know this truth when I was 12 years old at a Christian concert I attended with my sister. There, I heard for the first time that Jesus wants a friendship with me. He loves me SO much that He gave his life for me to save me from my sin, so I can know him in a close personal relationship now and for eternity. To have a friendship with the God of the universe was the best news I had ever heard, and I was so excited to ask Jesus into my heart. I began a friendship with Him that very day! Jesus became my anchor and I had no idea how significant that would be in my life with the storms that were to come. The anchor has definitely held in the midst of the worst of storms.

I also came to realize the amazing love that comes from a faithful friend—the kind of friend that Jesus is—and how laying down one's life is the greatest act of love and sacrifice. This truth became so real to me during our journey with Karina's cancer. She was in great need of blood—especially platelets. The leukemia was so aggressive that the donor blood was not staying with Karina; she would need a more perfect match for the blood/platelet transfusions she would need.

My husband and I were both tested to see if we would be a match… Ron turned out to be a perfect blood match and he began to give his blood/platelets on a regular basis. He actually holds the record at the Cascade Blood Bank for the most platelets given in such a short time. I realized how my husband laid down his life for our daughter—our precious daughter! It reminded me of the sacrifice Jesus made for us—God's special children, He sacrificed His blood on the cross for you and me, so we may live with Him now and forever in heaven. My husband's love for our daughter was amazing. He would give anything—his very life—for her to live. His sacrifice of his blood and platelets did bring life and strength to Karina—it was miraculous. (I was so thankful Ron was the match; to see the endurance and strength it took to donate that much blood was an incredible act of love!)

Jesus is literally dying to love on each one of us. He sacrificed His life for us in order that we may have a forever friendship with Him. That is amazing love and friendship!

Check Your Bearings

Jesus is our Friend. In fact, He wants to be our best friend. The definition of FRIEND from the dictionary is: "a person one knows and with whom one has a bond of mutual affection." And, "a person who helps support

Week One. JESUS IS OUR FRIEND

someone; companion, soul mate, confidant," are a few synonyms. The Hebrew meaning of friend is "one who loves."

True friendship is when someone knows you better than you know yourself and takes a position in your best interests in a crisis. Friendship goes beyond just sharing time together, and it is long lasting.

What are some qualities you think define a "best friend"?

I think some of the qualities that mark a best friend are: Honesty, Love, Humor, Empathy, Generosity, Trust, Loyalty, Encouragement, and Steadfastness.

What do these verses say about Jesus as a friend?

John 15:13-15

Romans 5:6-8

Hebrews 13:8

JESUS, OUR ANCHOR

John 16:33 _____

Joshua 1:9 _____

Matthew 11:28-30 _____

James 2:23 _____

Revelation 3:20 _____

Set the Anchor Truth in Your Heart

Look at John 11:17-44. What does this passage reveal about Jesus as our friend? _____

Jesus has so many qualities of a best friend. What aspects of human friendship have meant the most to you? Of Jesus' friendship? Can you think of

Week One: JESUS IS OUR FRIEND

a time He has been a comfort or encouragement to you, like a best friend would be?

Take some time to thank Him now for how He has been there for you as a forever best friend. If you can, write a few lines below of gratitude, expressing your heart to Him.

Having a friendship with Jesus brings Hope and Joy, and definitely anchors us in the storms of every day life:

> *"May the God of HOPE fill you with all JOY*
> *and Peace as you trust in Him…"*
> *Romans 15:13*

JESUS, OUR ANCHOR

Week One Notes:

WEEK TWO

Jesus Shows Us Our Father

*"See what great love the FATHER has lavished on us,
that we should be called children of God! And that is what we are!"*
1 John 3:1

Drop Anchor

I often think about my father and am thankful for his great love and care for me, both while I was growing up and as an adult. I realize some people do not grow up with such a positive image. My father wanted the best for me and would go out of his way to help me and encourage me.

A good earthly father is just a taste of our heavenly Father. My father loved me and provided for me, helped me and encouraged me. Some of my favorite father memories are when I was a little girl and he would carry me by piggyback upstairs to bed. His den door was always open to help me with my extremely challenging math story problems. He would come, seemingly at my beck and call, to fix a flat tire or a broken-down car, and in college he would help type my papers and work on art projects with me. My dad was available and caring, and that was definitely the way he showed his love for me. His qualities have given me just a glimpse of how the Lord cares for me as a Father.

The Lord is our Father. He loves us more than we can even imagine and desires a special relationship with you and me, His very special children. This was a new concept for the people of Israel in Jesus' time. Up until Jesus came, they knew God as their Creator, their Deliverer, their King, and their Judge, but . . . Father? *Daddy?* (*Abba*, as Jesus called Him, means "Daddy" in Hebrew.) This concept was new. And, it was one of the most important things Jesus came to teach us: He came to show us what our heavenly Father was really like. "He who has seen Me has seen the Father," Jesus said (John 14:9).

Check Your Bearings

The definition of FATHER from the dictionary is: "a man in relation to his natural child or children; one who cares for another." Good fathers are faithful, they take action, are teachers, bring hope, provide example, and are reliable. Good fathers are able to discern, and develop their children's hearts, souls, and minds.

Some earthly fathers have not provided a positive experience and make it hard to understand this character trait of the Lord. Our heavenly Father is the ultimate One; He gives us life both physically and spiritually—abundant life here on earth and life eternal. He is the perfect example of a loving, caring Father. He provides and cares for us; He helps us and carries us through this life.

Week Two. JESUS SHOWS US OUR FATHER

What are some words that describe a father to you?

What kind of earthly father example did you have growing up?

How do you think your experience with your earthly father influences your relationship with your heavenly Father?

What do the following verses say about the Lord as our Father?

John 1:12-13

John 10:29-30

Isaiah 9:6

JESUS, OUR ANCHOR

Matthew 6:9-13

Luke 11:9-13

1 Corinthians 8:5-6

Galatians 4:4-7

2 Corinthians 6:18

Romans 8:14-17

Matthew 7:9-11

Isaiah 64:8

Week Two. JESUS SHOWS US OUR FATHER

Set the Anchor Truth in Your Heart

Look at these verses. What do they say to you about the Lord's provision and care for you?

Matthew 10:29-31 _____
_____
_____

Matthew 6:26-27 _____
_____
_____

Luke 12:29-31 _____
_____
_____

Psalm 103:13 _____
_____
_____

Jesus cares for us and will never forget us. He will always provide for us!

Ron and I have experienced amazing confirmations to these verses many times over. Last spring, a sparrow flew into the dining room of our home. The little bird was stunned and shaking in the corner of the room. Ron cupped the little sparrow in his hand and fed it some sugar water in a spoon. The little bird's beak lapped up the water. It was a touching and poignant image of such frailty, held in a strong, caring hand. My husband set the little sparrow on the picnic table outside and encouraged it to fly. The bird didn't fly; instead it jumped back into the palm of his hand. Ron set it back on the table to go, but once again the bird jumped into his hand—not once but three times!! It was unbelievable!

JESUS, OUR ANCHOR

I commented, "I think this is a little message to us." We have had a very hard time since our daughter passed away and have sometimes wondered if the Lord really cares. This little sparrow reminded us of these verses and how much the Lord cares and will provide for and take care of us.

Can you think of a time when you have been discouraged and wondered if the Lord really cares for you? Are you facing something right now that makes you question His fatherhood?

_____
_____
_____
_____
_____

Share how these verses help to bring you truth and comfort. Which fatherhood trait means the most to you?

_____
_____
_____
_____
_____

Our Father knows best. When we spend time with the Lord and come to Him with faith like a little child He will pour out His love and care for us. Living anchored to this truth will help us live strong and confident in this life. Our Father loves us dearly and wants our complete trust.

Week Two. JESUS SHOWS US OUR FATHER

Week Two Notes:

WEEK THREE

Jesus Is Our Lord and Captain

"Trust in the Lord with all of your heart and lean not on your own understanding. In all your ways acknowledge Him and He will make your path straight."
Proverbs 3:5-6

Drop Anchor

I learned first hand what it's like to have a captain when Ron and I purchased a new boat and named it the "Karina Jean." The boat was a dream come true to use for hosting events and gatherings, with the hopes and prayers that all who boarded would be anchored in faith and friendships.

JESUS, OUR ANCHOR

The boat required a captain on board for several months while Ron "learned the ropes," so to speak. On our previous boat we ran everything ourselves, with no help from a captain, so this was a new experience for us. Having an official, certified captain on board the Karina Jean proved to be a great analogy for me in my faith and having Jesus as my Captain.

First of all, a captain knows best. The experience and wisdom of a captain are exceptional. A captain is well trained and an expert in operating boats and navigating the waters. We would meet with the captain daily to plan our day of cruising. The captain would guide us and straighten out our plans to be the most efficient and safe way.

A captain knows the destination and what it's going to take to get there. He is the expert in navigation, and I've learned to trust in his expertise. I can have a lot of my own plans, but he always knows best. I would call this time with our captain "pilothouse time." A pilothouse is an enclosed area on a boat containing the steering wheel, compass, and navigating equipment. I definitely liken this time to the need for similar time with Jesus on a daily basis to guide me in this life!

A captain is also able to fix things, and boats have a LOT of things that can go wrong. There is great comfort in knowing our captain can solve problems and restore broken systems. This too reminded me of how the Lord is able to fix and straighten things out, and help me with my life problems and challenges.

I've also come to "practice the presence" of the captain. He was always on the boat, and when he was in my sight I was on my best behavior. Having a captain in our midst helped heighten my awareness of how I treated my husband, and my own attitudes, actions, and words. I was more conscious of how Jesus is my captain aboard my life, and I wanted to be pleasing to Him in all I say or do. Also, it was comforting to know the captain was on board even when I couldn't see him. There was a feeling of security and confidence that we were always in good hands.

Week Three: JESUS IS OUR LORD AND CAPTAIN

Finally, a captain can be called on at any time. He is at my beck and call, ready and able to help, guide, and direct me to safe harbors. The captain analogy has really opened my eyes to being more aware of how Jesus is in my life as the ultimate Lord and Captain!

Check Your Bearings

LORD and CAPTAIN have similar definitions from the dictionary. LORD means someone having power, authority, or influence; leader, king, and commander are just a few synonyms. The word CAPTAIN means a commander, a person who is at the head of or in authority over others—chief, leader, or commander of a ship.

When we receive Jesus into our lives and believe in His truths, we allow Him to be the leader and "Lord and Captain" of our lives. He desires a relationship with each one of us to follow and trust Him with all of our hearts. He comes on board our lives to help us navigate it on the best course He has planned for us!

What comes to mind when you hear the word "Lord" or "Captain"?

What do the following verses say about Jesus our Lord and Captain?

Psalm 25:4-5

JESUS, OUR ANCHOR

James 1:5-6

Psalm 32:6-11

Psalm 16:7-8

Proverbs 2:6-9

Jeremiah 29:11-13

Isaiah 25:9

Proverbs 16:9

Psalm 9:10

Week Three. JESUS IS OUR LORD AND CAPTAIN

Set the Anchor Truth in Your Heart

Have you asked the Lord to "come on board" your life? Have you allowed Him to be the "Lord and Captain"? If so, describe what that has meant to you.

Do you have a regular time in your day that you can spend with the Lord to ask Him for His help and guidance (like a "pilothouse time")? What does that look like?

What helps you most during this time? What are some things that get in the way of this time?

There is a famous phrase about "practicing the presence of God." * What does the phrase "Practicing the Presence of the Captain (Jesus)" mean to you?

To realize we have the expert on life—Jesus—as our Captain, ready and waiting to meet and help us navigate our lives on daily basis, is amazing news!

* *The Practice of the Presence of God* is a famous book of collected teachings of Brother Lawrence (born Nicholas Herman), a 17th-century Carmelite monk, compiled by Father Joseph de Beaufort. The basic theme of the book is the development of an awareness of the presence of God.

JESUS, OUR ANCHOR

Look at the following verses and make a note of what they say about the Lord's guidance and care:

Mark 4:35-41

Isaiah 26:3-4

Psalm 73:23-24

Jeremiah 17:7-8

What are some situations you are facing in your life right now for which you need guidance and wisdom from the Lord? Are there any situations or relationships that need help "straightening out," like a Captain would do?

Week Three. JESUS IS OUR LORD AND CAPTAIN

Do you really trust Jesus as the Lord and Captain of your life? Why or why not? What do you sense He might be saying to you about that, in your heart?

_____
_____
_____
_____
_____
_____
_____
_____

This anchor truth set in your heart will bring a sure confidence and hope that are firm and secure. Your life has a captain when Jesus is on board. He gives directions, takes charge, and knows the dangers of the sea and can steer you around them, through and even over them!

Your life also has a course when Jesus is on board. Without Him, our lives are like ships on the sea, tossed about without compass or chart. We will drift with no purpose or direction. We must be willing to follow where He leads. We may not know, but He does and that is enough! We are in the best hands with Jesus as our Lord and Captain. He has an amazing journey for each one of us and promises us He will be with us the whole way!

JESUS, OUR ANCHOR

Week Three Notes:

WEEK FOUR

Jesus Is Our Shepherd

"The Lord is my shepherd; I shall not want. He makes me lie down in green pastures. He leads me beside still waters. He restores my soul. He leads me in paths of righteousness for his name's sake. Even though I walk through the valley of the shadow of death, I will fear no evil for you are with me; your rod and your staff, they comfort me."
Psalm 23:1-4

Drop Anchor
The first time I remember hearing the 23rd Psalm was when I was 16 years old, and they were words I will never forget. The psalm was read at the very first funeral I attended, for my friend's dad's untimely death. The words were comforting but a little confusing. I associated the psalm with death and stayed clear for a long time from ever reading it again. It wasn't a good memory, and it definitely left a negative mark on me.

JESUS, OUR ANCHOR

Many years passed and it wasn't until just a few years ago that I heard a message at The Anchor (our non-denominational monthly ministry gathering for women, to anchor them in faith and friendship), at our gathering in Bellevue, Washington. The speaker for the evening was a well-known news journalist who has been an anchor woman for KING 5 News in Seattle, on CBS and *Good Morning America*, as well as being recognized as the first Native American to file a report on a national news broadcast.

Her message began with the story of her early childhood. She grew up in a family of seven children and in severe poverty. She shared about how her aunt—a missionary—would come to visit each year, and would help her memorize the 23rd Psalm. She didn't understand what the words really meant, but anchored them in her heart anyway. The time spent with her aunt was very special and she never forgot it.

The words from Psalm 23 didn't make a difference in her life until she reached her mid-50s and her world came crashing down. She found herself alone and distraught one night in a New York hotel. On this one particular night—at her lowest, darkest moment of questioning the purpose of her life and the heartbreak she was enduring—she wondered, *Is there more to this life?* She had everything one would dream of in terms of extravagant, earthly security. But none of that was helping her now.

All of sudden the words of the 23rd Psalm came rushing back to her mind: "The Lord is my shepherd; I shall not want . . ." She knelt on the floor and asked the Lord to help, and to come into her life that night. An amazing peace and joy came over her that she could barely put into words. She was so thankful for the time and effort her aunt had put into helping her memorize that short passage from the Bible. The words of the 23rd Psalm came alive to her and she heard the Lord saying, "Follow me." The decision she made that night changed her life.

The 23rd Psalm began to speak to me as well in a very powerful way that night as I listened to this woman's message. I have just begun to discover the truth behind the precious words of Psalm 23 and now count it one of the most important anchor truths—the Lord is my Shepherd!

Check Your Bearings

A SHEPHERD is defined as "a person who herds, tends, and guards sheep; a person who protects, guides, or watches over a person or group of people."

The Lord as our Shepherd takes on great meaning for our lives when we decide to follow Him. The Lord leads and guides us and goes before us. He walks with us through all of life on the hills and in the valleys. He is always with us. He fights for us with His rod and staff and keeps us safe from enemy attacks and harm. He pulls us in with His shepherd's crook when we start to drift and wander off. The Lord our Shepherd carries us when we are weak and leads us to the best place for us. This is such a great analogy for us to begin to understand the love and care the Lord has for us. We are His sheep—and sheep need a shepherd!

What do the following verses say about Jesus as our Shepherd and us as His sheep?

John 10:1-13 _____

Psalm 28:9 _____

JESUS, OUR ANCHOR

Isaiah 40:11

Matthew 2:6

John 10:14-18

Hebrews 13:20-21

Exodus 14:14

Mark 6:34

Psalm 95:6-7

Week Four: JESUS IS OUR SHEPHERD

Set the Anchor Truth in Your Heart

What does it mean to you to have the Lord as your Shepherd? What are some of the shepherd qualities of Jesus you appreciate most in your life?

How do you relate to being a sheep? Do you really trust where the Lord is leading you? Why or why not?

How do you hear/sense/recognize the Lord's voice and know where He's leading?

The Shepherd leads us through hills and valleys. What are some of the valleys you have gone through or are going through right now? How do you sense the Lord is with you?

What do the following verses say to you about Jesus as our Shepherd?

Psalm 79:13

JESUS, OUR ANCHOR

Psalm 100:3-5

Isaiah 53:6

Luke 15:3-7

This anchor truth set in your heart will bring confidence and joy as you begin to know and fully trust your Shepherd, Jesus, to take care of you and lead you on the best path. He loves us all dearly, and is always there to guide and carry us through the hills and valleys of life. (If you get a chance, I encourage you to listen to the words of a favorite song of mine that reminds us again of His sovereign presence in our lives, "Hills and Valleys" by Tauren Wells.) Jesus is the Great Shepherd, and He desires us to follow Him all the days of our lives.

Week Four Notes:

WEEK FIVE

Jesus Is Our King

"You are a chosen people, a royal priesthood, a holy nation, a people belonging to God, that you may declare the praises of him who called you out of darkness into his wonderful light."
1 Peter 2:9

Drop Anchor

This past summer, I had an experience that helped to remind me of the awesome truth that Jesus is our King. We were on the Karina Jean, anchored in the Princess Louisa Inlet and tucked behind a little island called McDonald Island. It is our family's favorite anchorage, and we have made many special memories there. The waters are warm, surrounded by the glorious beauty of the mountains and forest, and it is close to our favorite Young Life camp—Malibu—where my husband and I first met.

JESUS, OUR ANCHOR

Malibu and the inlet are only accessible by boat or seaplane, so it makes it very remote and peaceful. A boater's destination, for sure! One of my most special memories of Karina is in this exact anchorage, during her last summer with us. She enjoyed wakeboarding behind the tender (dinghy) all over the inlet and just loved every minute of it.

One of the most important advantages of this anchorage for our family has been that it is the only place where you can get satellite for the TV to work. This enables our family to keep in touch with the news, sports, and, of course, some entertaining movies. On this particular evening last summer, we were snuggled up on the couch to watch TV and one of our family favorite movies came on, *Princess Diaries 2*.

I hadn't seen this movie since before Karina passed away. The *Princess Diaries* movies were always one of her favorites and mine too. So, seeing her favorite movie in this special place made it a very memorable time for me. As I sat there watching, I was flooded with memories of my special treasure, Karina, and I found myself teary-eyed the whole way through the movie.

Finally, it came to the last scene, when Mia becomes Princess of Genovia. She has actually been a princess of this country since birth but doesn't come to find that out until she is a teenager. As she realizes who she really is, and begins to learn what it means to be a princess, her life changes, and she begins to live with confidence, grace, and purpose.

Princess Mia leads a parade in her new country, and includes all the little girls and boys. She gives them tiaras and crowns, and a pep talk on how they are princesses and princes. She encourages them to walk like it, talk like it, and live like it—and to just have fun!

Something spoke to me that evening as I watched this scene. I needed to hear those words! First of all, I need to recognize the fact that I am a princess and the Lord is my King. I can forget that sometimes, and I think many people don't even know this truth. It is an important truth to anchor in our hearts. We have a King, Jesus, who adores us and laid His life down for us, who has great plans for each one of us and desires to have a relationship with us. I was filled with confidence that evening as I watched the movie. It reminded me of the truth that I am precious to the Lord and a princess in His eyes. As I set this truth in my heart and really believe it, a confidence takes over, and it has been a good reminder to me to trust Him as my King.

Check Your Bearings

The definition of a KING is "a sovereign ruler; a person regarded as the finest or most important; a leader, ruler, or crowned head." Jesus is our King, and we are part of His royal family. "Royal" means having the status of or being related to the King or crown. We each belong to the royal family, and once this truth of who we are sets in our hearts, we will begin to live with confidence and grace. When we allow Jesus to be ruler of our lives, He is sovereign over all, and as we begin to let this truth anchor in our hearts, we can rest in Him. We can trust Him with our lives and experience His amazing peace.

What do the following verses say about Jesus as our King?

1 Timothy 6:11-15

Luke 1:31-33

Psalm 24:7-10

JESUS, OUR ANCHOR

Zechariah 14:9 _____
_____
_____

Colossians 1:9-13 _____
_____
_____

Revelation 1:4-5 _____
_____
_____

Revelation 17:14 _____
_____
_____

Revelation 19:16 _____
_____
_____

Ephesians 1:18-23 _____
_____
_____

Set the Anchor Truth in Your Heart

Read Matthew 6:33 and note what it says about Jesus, our King. I have noticed that the important word in this verse encourages us to seek the Lord first. As we make it a top priority in our lives to know the Lord, we will sense His presence and love. The word seeKING has stood out to me—that, as we seek, we will see the King at work in our lives.

Week Five. JESUS IS OUR KING

What does it mean to you that Jesus is your King? Do you live confidently on this truth?

What do the following verses say about how Jesus sees us?

Deuteronomy 7:6

Isaiah 62:3

Zephaniah 3:17

Matthew 28:17-20

Do you have confidence knowing that you are part of the Lord's royal family—a princess/prince? How is this easy or difficult for you to imagine?

JESUS, OUR ANCHOR

How does this truth affect the way you live your life?

_____
_____
_____
_____
_____

What thoughts or circumstances get in the way of you believing this truth?

_____
_____
_____
_____

    This anchor truth that Jesus is our King can change the way we live, once it is really set in our heart and we believe on it. The Lord has chosen each one of us to be a part of His royal kingdom, and once we let Him rule in our hearts, we will begin to live in the full confidence and assurance of His great care for our lives. He has the sovereign plan and knows best. So, as we seek Him in relationship and trust in Him, we will see and experience the one true KING!

End of Study Wrap-Up

*"And now, just as you accepted Christ Jesus as your Lord,
you must continue to follow him. Let your roots grow down into him,
and let your lives be built on him. Then your faith will grow strong in the
truth you were taught, and you will overflow with thankfulness."*
Colossians 2:6-7, NLT

As we finish this study, I hope and pray you have been able to let some or all of these truths settle more deeply in your heart. It is my prayer that you may experience the amazing joy and abundant life living anchored in Jesus and His love, truths, and promises brings.

Below are a few questions I encourage you take some time with after completing this study. Really press deep into your own heart—your emotions, your thoughts, your decision-making arena, your priorities and values—everything. Follow up with some others in your group. Share answers, and pray for one another as you each commit to living anchored in Jesus.

JESUS, OUR ANCHOR

1. What anchors you amidst the storms of life? Has your answer to this question changed since you began this study? If so, how?

2. Which Anchor Truth is easiest for you to set in your heart?

3. Which Anchor Truth is the hardest for you to set in your heart?

4. What verse from this study that really speaks to you? Write it down here.

5. What does it mean to you and how do you think it could change you?

"Keep looking for Jesus. No matter how frightening the circumstances may be around us, Jesus is there. He will calm the seas of trouble in His time. Invite Jesus into the boat of your stormy life and your life will become calm. The most secure place to be is in God's will."
-Mrs. Charles E. (Lettie) Cowman
Streams in the Desert

ABOUT THE AUTHOR

Katie Robertson is a retired teacher who has devoted the current season of her life to speaking, mentoring, and serving in her community, bringing hope and inspiration for living a life anchored by faith in Jesus Christ. She is the author of *Anchored: Walking by Faith, Living in Hope, Remembering Karina*, and *Live Anchored: A Bible Study*.

Katie founded and directs The Anchor, a growing intergenerational ministry to anchor women in faith and friendships with multiple locations in the Pacific Northwest (and growing!). A graduate of the University of Washington, Katie is also a runner, artist, the mother of two grown children, and the delighted grandmother of a precious little girl.

Katie and her husband, Ron, live in Gig Harbor, Washington, where they continue to enjoy their seaside home and many adventures on their boat, the *Karina Jean*. They love to use their boat to encourage others to live anchored in their faith; they are actively involved in leader care, hosting Malibu Couples Weekends, Young Life ministry, and benefits for a variety of local non-profits.

Also available:

Anchored
BY KATIE ROBERTSON

When diagnosed with cancer as a young teen, Karina Robertson was powerfully strengthened by her relationship with Jesus. Karina's story of unshakeable faith is told through memories, photographs, and the handwritten prayer journal entries of both mother and daughter. *Anchored* is a story for anyone seeking a renewal of faith, a model for anchoring a child in faith, or encouragement in their relationship with the Lord. It is a story about loving well, being loved, and trusting that—no matter what happens—we are in God's hands, anchored in God's unfailing love.

My Sister and Me
BY ANNIKA ROBERTSON

In this charmingly illustrated story, a little sister celebrates the fun of having a big sister. Real life little sister Annika Robertson wrote and illustrated this book at the age of 13 for her big sister, Karina, just after donating her stem cells, which were a perfect match for her sister's transplant to fight her cancer. A portion of the proceeds of this book goes to the Fred Hutchinson Cancer Research Center in Seattle, Washington.

Our Special Treasure
BY KATIE ROBERTSON

The story of a mother's and father's love for their "special treasure" introduces the young child to God's love and to His plan for each of us. Bright, cozy illustrations give a child's-eye view of what it means to be loved unconditionally, and each page of the story comes with a Bible verse. At the end of the book, young readers will enjoy meeting the real little girl who inspired the story, and parents will find tried-and-tested tips for anchoring a child in faith.

Available at Amazon.com

www.ingramcontent.com/pod-product-compliance
Lightning Source LLC
Chambersburg PA
CBHW052120070526
44584CB00017B/2578